SHOPS &
SHOPPING

Recalling the history
of shopping in
Great Yarmouth
Gorleston and
the Villages

Colin Tooke

1

First Published in 2010
by
Colin Tooke
14 Hurrell Road
Caister-on-Sea
Great Yarmouth NR30 5XG

ISBN 978-0-9556013-3-0

Printed in England by Blackwell Print & Marketing
Charles Street, Great Yarmouth, Norfolk NR30 3LA

Contents

Acknowledgements

Once again many people have been forthcoming with images, information and help that has enabled me to compile this book. To these people I am very grateful. They include Peter Allard, Joan Fletcher, Helen Gallaway, Julie Grint, Alison Hall (NMAS), Professor Michael Harvey, Peter Hellingsworth, Len Hodds, Lesley Johnson, Peter Jones, Alec McEwen, the Watts family and Glenda Wells. As with previous books many of the images are taken from my own collection and with some of these it has been impossible to establish the true copyright. Anyone who has a claim to the copyright of an image used in this book is asked to contact me in writing.

The additional images have been individually credited to the generous people who have allowed me copy pictures from their collections or family albums. I also have to thank John Simmons for once again checking my text and to my wife Jan, for her constructive criticism and encouragement to complete the book.

'Phone **819**

G. LONGFIELD

147, KING STREET (*St.* *Opposite* *George's Church*)

SPECIAL EASTER OFFER OF

LADIES' PURE SILK HOSE

REINFORCED ART SILK at **2/6** per Pair

In All Colours   Usual Price **3/11** per pair

An Easter offer in 1930 by George Longfield's outfitters shop at 147 King Street. Today this is a supermarket, on the corner with Yarmouth Way.

INTRODUCTION

The country's small shops are being killed off by the rise of the large supermarkets and on-line shopping. Grocers, butchers, fishmongers, drapers and corner shops are just a few of the many small retail outlets that have disappeared from the nation's high streets as the large self-service stores take over. The same thing has happened in the villages where the general store was once the heart of the village. This book covers shopping and shops from the late nineteenth century to the present day and the images have been chosen to represent just some of the retailers that have disappeared from the town and a few of the nearby villages during that period.

For the benefit of readers who may have forgotten, and younger readers, it is necessary to record that from the sixteenth century to 'decimal day' on 15 February 1971 this country used an imperial monetary system of pounds, shillings and pence.

12 pence (d) = 1 shilling (s) often written as 1/-.
20 shillings = 1 pound.

The coins in circulation were a halfpenny, penny, threepence, sixpence, shilling, two shilling (florin) and two shillings and six pence (half-crown). Prior to 1961 a farthing, one quarter of a penny, was legal tender. Some large items were priced in guineas where one guinea was equal to one pound and one shilling. Paper money consisted of notes valued at 10 shillings, one pound and five pounds. Ten pound notes were introduced in 1964 and twenty pound notes in 1970.

This advertisement for Bairds, who had shoe shops in Regent Street and Bells Road in Gorleston, appeared in 1930.

THE EARLY SHOP

Today shopping, for most people, is part of normal everyday life but the shops as we know them have only existed since mid-Victorian times. Before then people bought their daily essentials, such as food, at open markets, the market place being the centre of trade. Fresh food was brought in daily from the market gardens, located to the north of the town outside the town wall, or by people from the surrounding villages who brought their produce to town on specific market days. The market had clearly defined trading areas, the butchers selling their meat in the butchery or shambles along the eastern side while fish was only sold in the fish market, an area now covered by part of the Market Gates shopping centre. Shoppers only bought what was required for immediate use.

In the eighteenth century, with a rapidly-increasing population and, as more consumer items became available, trade increased and goods began to be sold from the front rooms of buildings, where there was workshop and storage space at the rear and living accommodation above. These early shopkeepers only sold goods they had made or produced themselves. Those who did not have the necessary space sold their wares from outside their houses. People only shopped for necessities. For most people items such as clothing and furniture were made at home. In country districts the pedlar was a familiar sight, travelling from door to door with a selection of goods in a basket.

What today has become the shop window was then, particularly for butchers and fishmongers, an unglazed opening onto the street with a pair of horizontal shutters, one of which could be hooked up to provide a shelter while the other formed a counter, the shop front. Windows eventually replaced these open fronts; small panes of glass set in a bowed window frame until, in the nineteenth century, sheet glass became widely available and large

This shop of Thomas Sparham, 74 Middlegate Street, was typical of shop fronts before large sheets of glass were available for windows. In the 19th century many builders and carpenters 'undertook' funeral work. Later this became a separate business and the Undertaker appeared.

windows could be created without the obstruction of glazing bars. Many butcher's shops however continued to have open fronts into the twentieth century. The shop window now became important to display effectively the shopkeepers' goods. Several of these early shop fronts, with bay windows and small panes of glass, were to be seen in the town well into the twentieth century, particularly in Middlegate Street and Howard Street.

From the 1850s developing technologies allowed the mass production of many foods and other items, including ornaments and household labour saving devices. Shopping in the Victorian Age became an accepted leisure pursuit, particularly with women looking for clothes. During the nineteenth century the population of this country doubled and, by the turn of the century, the

In the 16th century the 'flesh shambles' developed on the east side of the Market Place. Here all the town butchers were required to sell their meat. The wooden canopies in this picture of the 1870s gave some shelter to both customers and the open windows. In 1912 there were still five butchers shops in this row, now the site of Argos. The building on the right, on the corner of Market Gates, is the Bull public house, taking its name from this area of the market where bulls were once baited.

This shop of Charles Hunn, Yarmouth Road, Caister, seen here in the 1920s, is a typical example of the open fronted butcher's shops previously mentioned. The meat hangs in the open, labelled with its source. Today this is the shop of Caister Hardware.

9

expanding British Empire meant commodities from across the globe were available; the new department store developed from the earlier bazaar as a place where a large number of speciality lines were sold under one roof. The foundations of a consumer society had been laid. The Victorian Age also saw the heyday of the small corner shop, which became an important social meeting place for local communities. As many food stuffs would not keep for any length of time, the housewife went shopping almost every day. Few groceries were ready packed, meaning a long wait while each item was weighed and packed, giving the housewife ample time to chat and gossip.

In the mid-seventeenth century there was a severe lack of small change and many shopkeepers issued tokens. These tokens were issued to customers as small change and shopkeepers would often honour each other's tokens. There were at least forty-one issuers of tokens in the town at that time, including five bakers, six grocers, a hosier and a glover. A similar problem with small change occurred again in the late eighteenth century and again

tokens were issued. In the late nineteenth century a few tokens were issued by shopkeepers in the town as advertisements, or for use similar to later dividend stamps or the modern loyalty cards used by supermarkets. The Yarmouth shops to issue these were F Mayston, a grocer and tea dealer, S Lessey, also a grocer and tea dealer, and Robert Bumpstead, a grocer in the Market Place (whose token is shown here). Bumpstead's shop later became Barnes grocery shop, 8 Market Place, and today is a menswear shop, on the corner of the Conge.

The twentieth century brought great changes to the way people shopped. The first big change came with the Second World War when shoppers had to cope with extensive rationing of food and clothes as well as a severe shortage of other consumer goods. Ration books had been issued nationwide in November 1939 and the system began in January 1940 when butter, bacon, ham and sugar were the first food items to be rationed. Ration book holders were required to register with particular retailers and queues became a normal part of every-day shopping. As the war progressed more food items were rationed, many remaining on ration until well after the war had finished. In 1941 the rationing system was extended to cover clothes and, together with the shortage of almost all household goods, housewives now learned how to 'make do and mend'.

Bacon and Ham, rationed January 1940 to July 1954
Meat, rationed March 1940 to July 1954
Tea, rationed July 1940 to October 1952
Cheese, rationed May 1941 to May 1954
Soap, rationed February 1942 to September 1950
Sweets, rationed July 1942 to February 1953
Clothes, rationed June 1941 to May 1949

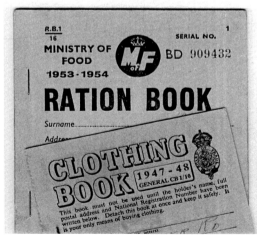

Several items were not rationed, including cosmetics and toilet preparations. This was in an effort to boost morale. Production of these items was, however, strictly controlled and this led to shortages in the shops and the inevitable growth of the black market.

The 1950s saw a change in shopping habits with the advent of self-service shops and later the supermarket. The days of the small corner shop were numbered. The first self-service shop in the town was Elmo's in the market place, which opened in 1959.

As an incentive to attract custom a few shops began to issue stamps in 1958, the most popular of which were Green Shield stamps, where one stamp was given for each 6d (2.5p) spent. The popularity of these stamps increased in 1963 when Tesco stores began to issue them. Tesco stores became the largest outlets for the stamps until they decided to stop issuing them in 1977. Other stamps issued by smaller shops included Gold Bond stamps and S&H Pink stamps.

Green Shield catalogue shops were established where books of stamps could be exchanged for a large range of goods. The stamps began to lose their popularity in the 1970s and in 1973 the catalogue shops were rebranded Argos, and another new form of retailing had arrived on the High Street.

The first of the national supermarket names to arrived in the town was Fine Fare, who opened in the old Woolworth store in Regent Road in 1962. In 1976 they took over Downsway in the Market Place. This had originally been called Downs, opening in 1966, but the name had changed to Downsway in 1975. This store was next to Palmers and is today a clothes store called M&Co. Tesco opened their first store in the Market Place in 1964 (a shop that is now Argos). In July 1980 they moved to a newly-built store, opened by comedian Russ Abbott, on Church Plain, (now the Palace Casino). This store closed in October 2003 when Tesco moved to their larger out-of-town store.

Sainsbury's opened in September 1975 in the new Market Gates shopping centre. In October 1989 they moved to a new store in St Nicholas Road, built on the site that was once Grout's silk factory. The original Sainsbury store is now Wilkinsons. The last of the big supermarkets to arrive in the town was Asda, whose new store at Vauxhall, built on the old railway goods yard, opened in April 1984.

TRADE SIGNS

The owners of inns and public houses have always attracted custom by displaying a sign outside their premises and, as the number of shops increased in the eighteenth century, the new shopkeeper found it necessary to follow suit. With a population, that was largely illiterate at that time, it was essential to advertise the type of shop with an easily-recognisable sign. Trade signs appeared, many projecting out over the street, displaying a symbol of the goods on offer at that establishment. Generally each trade carried the same type of sign. There were not as many signs in Great Yarmouth as were to be found in the larger towns and cities but the traditional signs, like the three golden balls of the pawnbroker (a sign still in use today) and the red and white striped pole of the barber, were to be seen on many premises. The apothecary or herbalist would advertise his trade by placing large glass jars filled with brightly-coloured liquid in the window; again a display sometimes still seen today in chemist shops.

A large wooden key hung over the hardware shop of George Sill in the Market Palace and a group of musical instruments over the façade of Watts' music shop in King Street. Most jewellers and clock makers had a clock outside their shop, as Samuels in King Street still have. Many of the town's trade signs of the nineteenth century were removed as shops were altered and changed and were preserved on display in the old Tolhouse Museum but unfortunately these were all lost during the Second World War when the museum was bombed.

A trade sign still to be seen in the town is the large fishing float above the pavement outside Pownall's fishing tackle shop in

Left: The trade sign of George Sill's shop in the Market Place. A key, often gilded, was the traditional sign for a ironmongers or a hardware shop. *Right:* the musical instruments above Arthur Watt's shop in King Street. This 'Golden Fiddle' as it became known, dated from 1864 and remained in position when the shop became Wolsey & Wolsey in 1910

The tobacconist shop at 17 & 18 Broad Row, established in the late eighteenth century as a snuff shop. For many years it was Blyth's and later Norton's. The Highlander had stood there for almost two hundred years before being removed in the 1970s to a snuff museum in Sheffield.

14

Regent Road. A few doors away, fixed to the wall above Doughty's sports shop on the corner of Regent Road and Nelson Road was a giant tennis racket, but this has now disappeared.

Picture courtesy of Norfolk Museum & Archaeology Service.

Perhaps the most well-known trade sign in the town was the Highlander outside the tobacconist shop of Norton's (at one time Blyth's) in Broad Row. This life-size wooden figure, which dated from the early nineteenth century, stood guard beside the doorway until the 1970s. Another, similar figure was to be found inside the shop, originally from Springall's tobacconist shop a few doors away, a business taken over by Norton's. The Highlander had been a traditional trade sign for shops selling snuff, a very popular commodity in the nineteenth century. At one time it was possible to sample the snuff by taking a pinch from a small container in the hand of the Highlander.

The figure that stood outside the shop in Broad Row had had an adventurous life during the fishing season, often finding itself mysteriously transported to the Fishwharf during the hours of darkness. The figure now resides peacefully in the snuff factory of Wilson & Co. in Sheffield, where he is well looked after. The other figure (left) was, after being restored, on display for a few years in the Tolhouse Museum and is now in a museum store, patiently awaiting a suitable position.

One of the last trade signs in the town was removed in 2009, the King Herring above the Bloater Depot in Regent Road. This was removed when the shop changed its name to Fish'n Chick'n. The sign is now on display in the Time and Tide Museum, Blackfriars Road.

Another form of advertising that was common in the nineteenth century was the 'doorway advertisement' where the name of the shop was spelled out in mosaic tiles in the entrance. Over the years these have largely disappeared as shops have been altered but one fine example still exists in the town today, in the doorway of a café in George Street. This was the original shop of Aldreds the jewellers, a firm established in 1795. Aldred & Son made and installed many of the large public clocks in the town, including the Town Hall clock (1882) and the Newtown Methodist Chapel (1907).

On the façade of a shop at 25 Northgate Street is a wooden bull's head, put there when it was Bell's butcher's shop. The head was restored in 2000 and, although the premises are now a restaurant, the trade sign remains in place.

When postcards became popular in Edwardian times they were often given away as advertisements, as this example dated 1909. The tailors and outfitters Doughty & Baker, whose shop was on White Horse Plain, now Cox the jewellers, used the cards to promote the extension to their January sale. The cards had a picture of the shop on the other side.

(Glenda Wells)

(Alec McEwen)

Another form of advertising was the wall advert. These were painted directly onto the walls of buildings and were once a common sight. The printed billboard led to the decline of wall-painted signs and few survive today. These 'ghost signs' as they are now called provide a window into the past and evidence of the craftsmanship that once went into their production. Some advertised household names such as Bovril or Nestles Milk while other were very local. The example illustrated here, photographed in the 1990s, was painted on a wall in Nelson Road Central, directing customers to Larke's shop in King Street.

17

A BIT
OF
— Old —
Yarmouth.

Clowes'
Stores
IN THE
EARLY YEARS
OF THE
VICTORIAN ERA.

1837.		1897.	
Per lb.		Per lb.	
Tea - from 6/4 to 14/-	☞	Tea - from 1/- to 2/4	
Sugar - „ 6d. „ 1/0	☞	Sugar - „ 1d. „ 2½d.	
Currants - „ 8d. „ 1/-	☞	Currants - , 2d. „ 5d.	
Raisins - „ 9d. „ 1/-	☞	Raisins - „ 3d. „ 5d.	
Sultanas - - 1/4	☞	Sultanas - - - 3d.	
Peel - - - 1/4	☞	Peel - - - 4d.	
Nutmegs - - - 8/-	☞	Nutmegs - - 3/2	
Butter - - 2/-	☞	Butter 10d. choicest 1/-	
Pepper - - 2/8	☞	Pepper (The Finest) - 1/-	
Candles (The Old-Fashioned "Dip") 8d.	☞	Candles (Wax) - 3d.	
Soap - „ 6d. „ 8d.	☞	Soap - „ 2d. „ 3d.	
Soda 1/6 per stone.	☞	Soda 6d. per stone.	

CLOWES' STORES,

To mark Queen Victoria's Diamond Jubilee in 1897 Clowes, the high-class grocers with branches at 15 Hall Quay and in Gorleston High Street, advertised the price difference of several commodities over the sixty years of Victoria's reign. It would appear that the price of many items had dropped during the Victorian era. Clowes later opened a branch in Martham.

THE ARCADES

In 1902 the first retail shops to appear on the Marine Parade opened in a new Marine Arcade, built on the site of Ansell Place, which ran from the Parade through to Apsley Road. The arcade had a domed glass roof and there were twenty shops of all different trades, many of them run by leading businesses in the town. All were lit by electricity, a new feature that many town centre shops did not have until several years later. Two years later another arcade was built beside the first, both having decorative terracotta frontages with the dates at the top. In 1911 the Empire Picture Theatre was built on the northern side of the second arcade.

By the 1920s several other shops had opened along the Marine Parade but the Arcades remained popular and by now contained a large variety of shops, the largest being the five units occupied by Palmers department store. Another five units were taken by May & Co., jewellers. The other shops were selling goods that were typical of seaside souvenir shops, such as Josefina's Emporium of fancy goods, Ralph Keymer, a fancy draper and Middleton's bazaar. Spall's fancy goods occupied three units and others businesses included George Tadda and J M Habesch (both oriental bazaars), Mrs Sulway (a Venetian bead shop), and Madame Sato (a palmist).

These decorative mosaic tiles still exist in the pavement at what was the Apsley Road entrance to one of the Arcades

One of the Marine Arcades in the 1920s. Note the high, domed glass roof.

The entrance to the Marine Arcade from Apsley Road.

A restaurant, a tobacconist and a confectionery shop completed the wide range of shops in the two arcades, many traders having shops in both the north and south arcades.

By the 1970s the shops had all gone, the south arcade had become the Marine Arcade Restaurant and the north arcade was the Stagecoach Amusements. Today both arcades form the Leisureland Amusements, but above the modern plastic façade can still be seen the original Edwardian terracotta work with the dates 1902 and 1904.

In 1925 work began to construct an arcade of shops in the town centre. Built by the local builder B G Beech, the Central Arcade ran behind Regent Street. Many buildings were demolished, including all those in Row 74, and the jewellery and watchmakers' shop of Aldred & Sons in King Street. The arcade opened in May the following year with nineteen businesses on the south side and seventeen on the north, many occupying more than one of the seventy-six units.

Aldreds jeweller's shop had been rebuilt, now forming the southern corner of the arcade entrance from King Street. In the early 1970s the shops on the south side of the arcade included the café of Notarianni, Dr Scholl's foot comfort service, Archway estate agents, Seaforths travel agency, Gray's the opticians, the Singer Sewing Machine shop, Kob's newsagents and toy shop and, on the corner with Regent Street, the Arcade Florist. On the north side the shops included Kay Crawford's fashion shop, the Yarmouth Wool shop, Hellingsworth's ladies outfitters and Henry Pike's tobacconists, the smallest shop in the arcade. The shoe shop of Freeman, Hardy & Willis was on the corner with King Street, a site that had been a shoe shop for over one hundred years until the recent closure of Shoe Express. Many of the businesses mentioned above traded in the Arcade for several years. In 1987 the arcade was modernised and renamed the Victoria Arcade and in recent years many of the long-established shops have been replaced by new names.

Shopping in the Arcade.

Above in the Central Arcade in April 1967 and left in the renamed Victoria Arcade in June 2001.

THE ROWS

The Rows of the town, of which 145 were numbered in 1804, were mainly residential although in some rows industrial premises such as warehouses, fish curing houses, bakeries and iron foundries were to be found. There were few shops in these rows except in Row 130, previously known as St Peter's Row or Old White Lion Row, named after the public house on the south-east corner. This row ran from King Street to Middlegate and there were a few shops on the southern side, which today forms the southern pavement of Nottingham Way. These shops included a greengrocer, fishmonger, hairdresser and boot maker. No records have survived of any shops that may once have existed in any of the other numbered rows.

Two rows, not included in the 1804 numbering scheme, had by that time become well-known and established as shopping areas. These were Market Row and Broad Row. For many years these rows had been an accepted route for carts travelling from the Hall Quay to the Market Place but, in 1784, Market Row was blocked to carts by erecting an old cannon at the western end. The row was then paved and soon became a favourite place for shops. By the nineteenth century both rows were recognised as a main shopping area. In the 1870s there were 28 shops in Broad Row, including two tobacconists, two jewellers, three ironmongers, and nine shops selling clothing and linen. Shops that traded in goods that would not be found today, but were typical of the time, included a straw hat and bonnet maker, an umbrella maker and a brushmaker.

Above: Plattens shops in May 1988, on the north side of Broad Row. The firm also had a shop in Gorleston.

Left: The Home & Colonial Stores, 11 Broad Row, traded until 1962. The shop later became part of Plattens store. Next to the Home & Colonial was the jeweller's shop of Engledow and Gallant.

24

Broad Row looking west in 1923. Stead & Simpson had a shoe shop on each corner of the row. The shop on the left later became Bradley's and was then demolished, now the open space on the corner with Howard Street.

In February 1973 the shops on the right of the above picture were Visionhire, the Surplus Trading Company and Norfolk Radio, on the corner with Howard Street.

In 1889 the family firm of Plattens opened their first shop in
Broad Row. Originally tailors and outfitters the business
expanded into furniture, carpets and hardware, taking over
adjacent shops until almost half the northern side of the row
became Plattens department store. With a grocery shop and two
smaller shops on the other side of the row, Plattens became the
largest trader in Broad Row. With the retirement of the grandson
of the founder, the firm ceased trading in September 1998. In
1896 Boots the chemist, who already had a shop in Regent Street,
opened a branch at 2 Broad Row; this shop closed in 1969. For
many years at number 11 Broad Row was one of the town's
leading jewellers and watchmakers, Engledow & Gallant.

Market Row had been 'stopped up for the convenience of foot
passengers' and during the nineteenth century became a busy
shopping area. By the 1870s there were 38 shops in Market Row,
most of them selling essential items such as grocery and clothing.
There were also two china and glass dealers and two fancy
repositories, one owned by William Humphrey and the other by
Lucinda Hasler. In 1903 the family firm of Bretts, who had been
in business since the 1860s, opened a furniture shop on the
southern corner of Market Row and Howard Street. In 1960 the
shop on the opposite corner, which earlier had been Arnold's,
then Brenner's and later Peacock's Bazaar, was taken over by
Bretts. The firm later expanded along Howard Street, taking in
what had been the Blue House public house. In recent years much
of this property has been rebuilt, still a furniture shop on the
south side of the row and now a social housing complex on the
north side.

In the 1970s the traders in Market Row included well-known
names such as Courts furnishers, Elsey's outfitters, Hannant's toy
and model shop, Cooper's tool department, Matthes cake shop
and tea rooms and Olivette's wool shop.

The shop with the longest trading history in the row was R. T.
Martins, the outfitters, who were there for over one hundred
years. On the corner with the Market Place was Vettese's

restaurant, later the Ventura restaurant, above Hepworths (later the Abbey Building Society, now Santander). In 1929 Brant's drapery shop took over George Carr's business at 4, 5, 6 and 7 Market Row. On 12 January 1938 a disastrous fire destroyed most of the building which then had to be demolished. The new building was set back a few feet to allow the row to become wider at that point and in 1970 it was taken over by Court's Ltd, as a furniture store. On 13 September 1995 fire once again destroyed this building, together with several other smaller shops. Fought by over 100 fire fighters, the blaze destroyed property on both sides of the row, including the well-known butcher's shop of Greenacre's. It was to be many years before the properties on the north side of the row were rebuilt, those on the opposite side still waiting.

For many years the fish curing firm, John Woodger & Sons, had a shop at 2 Market Row. Another well-known shop in the row was that of Fieldings Ltd, cycle and radio dealers. Fieldings opened in Market Row in 1921 and by 1937 had two shops, numbers 35 and 36, on the south side. Fieldings closed in 1973.

Bevingtons, 34 Market Row, was a well-known chemist shop which opened in the late 1940s. This had previously been an outfitters and then a shoe shop (see next page).

As a chemist shop, between Olivettes and Fieldings, Bevington's traded for many years. Today it is a teashop.

27

R. & T. MARTINS,

Tailors, Hatters, Hosiers & Outfitters,

MARKET ROW, YARMOUTH.

Selected New Materials of the Best Manufacture

FOR

SUITS, COATS, TROUSERS & VESTS.

∴ Silk and Felt Hats. ∴

FLANNEL TENNIS and BOATING SHIRTS.

FORD'S "EUREKA" SHIRTS.

FOOTBALL HOSE, SWEATERS, AND JERSEYS.

GENTLEMEN'S UNDERCLOTHING in = =
SANITARY WOOL, MERINO, COTTON, etc.

Waterproof Garments of Guaranteed Make.

GENTLEMEN'S ALPACA AND SILK UMBRELLAS. ∴. SCARVES, TIES, AND
GLOVES IN GREAT VARIETY.

Above: Sayer the tailor and outfitter at 34 Market Row. In the 1930s this became Stead & Simpson's shoe shop and later Bevingtons the chemists. Today it is a tea room.

Left: R&T Martin, another tailor and outfitter, traded at 27 and 28 Market Row for over one hundred years. In the 1890s they were described as one of the best tailoring businesses in the town. There was a workshop at the rear for their bespoke tailoring service.

Above: The butcher's shop of Greenacre in October 1993. This was one of the shops destroyed in the fire of 1995. The business moved to the Market Place but has since closed.

Left: Market Row in 1989 looking towards Howard Street. Tangle Free Plus, Tracy Fashions and Traddles have all now ceased trading.

A family business that began in Market Row and quickly expanded to other parts of the town was the chain of wool shops that traded under the name of Olivettes. Founded in April 1931 by Olive Gillingwater the first shop opened at 32 Market Row. The following year Olive married Alfred Harvey and during the 1930s other shops were opened in Regent Road, Marine Arcade and King Street. The war forced the closure of these shops except Market Row. The King Street shop was a victim of the bombing in 1941.

After the war, and now joined in the business by her husband, Olive expanded again by taking in the shops either side of 32 Market Row. In 1955 a shop was opened in Gorleston High Street next to the Coliseum cinema and two years later a branch at Caister. From 1961 until 1966 there was an Olivettes at 1a Salisbury Road and in the 1960s shops in Bells Road, Gorleston and High Mill Road, Southtown were opened. In addition to wool sales the shops were well-known for their large range of babies and children's wear.

In 1979 the main shop moved from Market Row to 12 and 13 Broad Row. Olivettes ceased trading in February 1994.

Olive and Alfred Harvey outside their new shop in Broad Row in 1979.
(Michael Harvey)

30

Left: A window display in Olivettes Market Row shop in the 1950s. At this time knitting was very popular with many women.

(*Michael Harvey*)

Below: Two adverts for adjacent shops in the row, Turner's confectionery shop at number 15 and Daniel's at number 16.

O. TURNER,

Pastrycook & Confectioner

15, MARKET ROW,

GREAT YARMOUTH.

Bride Cakes a Speciality.   French and Swiss Pastry Fresh Daily.

PARTIES AND SCHOOL TREATS SUPPLIED.

Birthday, Christening & all kinds of Cakes

A LARGE ASSORTMENT OF FANCY

CONFECTIONERY, CHOCOLATES, ETC.

NOTE—15, MARKET ROW.

CHRISTMAS FRUITS.

FOR THE CHOICEST & CHEAPEST NO PLACE LIKE

DANIELS'

16, MARKET ROW.

ORANGES, NUTS, FIGS, RAISINS, GRAPES, PRUNES, MUSCATELS, IMPERIAL PLUMS, PORTUGAL ONIONS, &c.

A CONSTANT SUPPLY OF GOOD EGGS

AT THE LOWEST POSSIBLE PRICES.

COCOA NUTS IN ALL SIZES & LARGE QUANTITIES

Always kept in Stock.

Early in the Spring, choice varieties of Kitchen Garden Seeds, Bedding Plants, Roses, &c.

THE TRADE SUPPLIED.

NOTE THE ADDRESS :—

16, MARKET ROW,

GREAT YARMOUTH.

AGENT FOR DANIEL BROS., NORWICH.

Left: A mid-Victorian advert for a shop in Market Row. This comes from a 1862 copy of the Yarmouth Independent newspaper.
This was at a time when farthings were important currency, particularly in the drapery trade. Note the polite wording of the advert.

ARNOLDS

In May 1869 two brothers, Frank and William Arnold, purchased the drapery and silk merchants shop of J. R.Cossons, at 180 King Street. The business was soon expanded with the purchase of the adjacent shops at 179 and 181 King Street and by 1886 carpets and furniture had been added to the growing list of items sold.

In 1889 they took over a shop in Market Row, on the north-west corner with Howard Street, previously the business of Mr H.Lay, a draper's and carpet warehouse. This became Arnolds furniture and carpet warehouse, the King Street shops concentrating on the drapery and silk side of the business. In 1897 Arnold Brothers were advertising themselves as 'Drapers, Silk Mercers, Carpet Warehousemen and House Furnishers at King Street, Market Row and Howard Street'.

By the turn of the century Arnolds had taken over the business of Frederic Fuller on the corner of Regent Street and King Street, 'The Gt. Yarmouth Dress House', specialising in silks, dress fabrics and costumes. Arnolds now had shops at 1&2 Regent Street and 178 to 181 King Street, a large corner site suitable for redevelopment.

The shops at 178 King Street and 1 & 2 Regent Street were demolished in 1905 and a new corner store built on the site, opening on 19 May 1906, also taking in the original shops at 179 to 181 King Street.

William Arnold died in 1903 and Frank in 1916. The business was then run by William's sons Spencer and Percy. By 1909 the furniture shop in Market Row had become Arnolds china and furniture department but closed the following year, later to

ARNOLD BROTHERS,

Drapers, Silk Mercers,

Carpet Warehousemen,

— House Furnishers,

King Street,
Market Row, Howard Street,
G T. Y A R M O U T H.

King Street Drapery Establishment.

ARNOLD BROTHERS take the opportunity of the Jubilee Supplement of the *Independent* to thank the public of Great Yarmouth and Neighbourhood for the constantly increasing support they have received since the commencement of their business in 1869.

During these 28 years ARNOLD BROS. have made constant and important additions to their premises, which are now most convenient for carrying on their large Drapery Business.

The **Newly-arranged DRESS DEPARTMENT** occupies an important space, has a splendid Light and is Stocked with a great variety of inexpensive and choice **Dress Materials.**

The **Millinery, Mantle, and Ladies' Outfitting Show-rooms** will well repay a visit. Latest Novelties at Moderate Prices.

Manchester and Cloth Departments, noted for Useful and Cheap Goods, constantly in demand.

Lace Curtains and Muslins a Speciality.

Floorcloth and Linoleum Hall, Carpet Warehouse, Linen, Cretonne, and Quilts. ARNOLD BROS. have always given these Departments great care and attention, and are able to offer these Goods at Low Prices.

All **Fancy Drapery Departments,** as **Hosiery, Gloves, Lace, Umbrellas, Trimmings, Haberdashery, Ties,** and **Scarves,** always well assorted.

ARNOLD BROTHERS'
Furniture ‡ Warehouses.

The Largest Stock of ——
Household Furniture in Yarmouth.

THESE commodious Premises, in which was carried on for so many years a large Carpet and Drapery Business, are most convenient for the Furniture Trade, affording ample floor space for the display of a large assortment.

Dining-room, Drawing-room, & Bedroom Suites,
Bedsteads, Bedding,
And all kinds of Useful & Inexpensive Furniture.

ESTIMATES GIVEN FOR
Furnishing Hotels, Restaurants,& Boarding Houses.

Market Row & Howard Street Furniture Warehouse.

iv

An Arnolds advertisement in Queen Victoria's Diamond Jubilee year, 1897. The top picture shows the shops in King Street and at the bottom the shop on the Market Row/Howard Street corner.

The horse-drawn delivery vehicle of Arnolds. Note the smart military-style
uniforms of the delivery men.

The linen and furnishing department in Arnolds new corner store which sold
'household lines of every description'.

become Brenner's Bazaar and in more recent years part of Brett's furniture shop as described earlier.

On 1 February 1919 the King Street store, several small shops further west in Regent Street and cottages in Row 66 were totally destroyed by fire, one of the largest fires ever seen in the town. The fire broke out at 9.30 p.m. on a Monday night and quickly spread throughout the building, the limited resources of the fire brigade unable to have much effect. The two local fire engines were supplemented by the port tug, *George Jewson*, which moored at Hall Quay and pumped water up Regent Street. An additional engine arrived from Norwich some hours after the fire had started but by now it was too late to save anything. One reason given for the rapid spread of the fire was the amount of timber used in the construction of the building in 1905. It was estimated at the time that the total damage came to £100,000, a sum that today would equal over £8.5 million. Rebuilding started almost immediately, and a new store opened on the corner site in 1922. The Regent Street frontage of the new store was built five feet further back, to allow the street to be widened at this point.

The second floor restaurant was advertised as 'the shoppers rendezvous, luncheons served daily in charming surroundings'. In 1936 the business was sold to the Debenham group, but the store continued to trade under the old family name of Arnolds.

In the Second World War; in 1941, the basement was converted into an auxiliary hospital with 50 beds and a well-equipped operating theatre, used for the duration of the war.

The restaurant was always a popular venue for private parties, receptions and dinner-dances. Many local clubs and organisations, such as the Rotary Club, used it as a regular meeting place. In 1953 Arnolds 'Regency Restaurant' was offering the 'best three-course lunch in town' for 2/6 (12½p). A self-service cafeteria was opened in the basement, one of the first in the town.

In December 1972 the name of the store changed to 'Debenhams' and the well-known name of Arnolds, which had

The corner store which opened on 19 May 1906 and was destroyed by fire on 1 February 1919.

Arnolds new store which opened in 1922. Today the King Street frontage is divided into three smaller retail units.

existed in the town for over one hundred years, disappeared from the local retail scene. The shop continued to trade on similar lines as in previous years but, in June 1985, the store closed with the loss of 150 jobs. The building was then divided into three smaller units which today are Topshop, Superdrug and River Island. Today the large white building standing on the corner of King Street and Regent Street has one reminder of the old family firm, the letter 'A' still visible on the stonework between the windows on the second floor.

On 30 October 2008 Debenhams returned to the town, opening a new department store in the newly-extended Market Gates shopping centre.

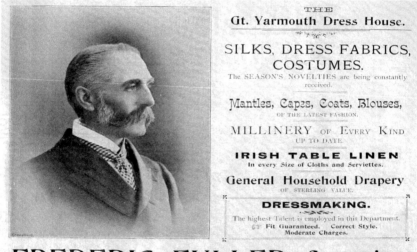

THE
Gt. Yarmouth Dress House.

SILKS, DRESS FABRICS, COSTUMES.
The SEASON'S NOVELTIES are being constantly received.

Mantles, Capes, Coats, Blouses,
OF THE LATEST FASHION.

MILLINERY OF EVERY KIND
UP TO DATE.

IRISH TABLE LINEN
In every Size of Cloths and Serviettes.

General Household Drapery
OF STERLING VALUE.

DRESSMAKING.
The highest Talent is employed in this Department.
Fit Guaranteed. Correct Style. Moderate Charges.

FREDERIC FULLER, Costumier,
1 & 2, Regent Street, & 178, King Street, Gt. Yarmouth.

Frederic Fuller, whose large three storey shop on the corner of King Street and Regent Street was taken over by the Arnold brothers to enable them to rebuild the corner site into their department store. Mr Fuller advertised "ample staffs of polite and experienced assistants are employed, and owing to the first-class facilities in use the largest and most important order receives prompt and efficient care".

BAZAARS

In the last few years there has been a proliferation of shops selling low price goods, all at one price, usually one pound. With names such as Pound Land and The Pound Shop they have appeared on the nation's High Streets. In Great Yarmouth there are several such shops today, some national chains, while others are small individual retailers. Some trade as 99p shops and one, trading as Pound Crazy in the Market Place in 2009, became a 97p shop, seeking to undercut rivals.

These are the modern equivalent of the early twentieth century bazaars, a term not often used by the retail trade today. The original 'Penny Bazaar' was started in the nineteenth century by Michael Marks, on a market stall in Leeds where he sold everything on his stall for one penny. After a few years this business developed into Marks & Spencer, with Penny Bazaars being opened in many towns across the country. In 1911 their first shop in Great Yarmouth, a penny bazaar, was opened in George Street, opposite Broad Row. In 1932 M & S moved to King Street, taking over the department store of Boning Brothers, a site where they still trade today. In 2009 M&S re-introduced the 'Penny Bazaar' for a short while to mark their 125th anniversary.

F.W.Woolworth & Co. came to this country from America in 1909, opening a chain of 3d and 6d stores. Their first shop in Great Yarmouth opened in Regent Road, in 1925. In 1937 they were still selling 'nothing over 6d'.

There were several smaller shops classed as bazaars in the town, including Brenner's Bazaar, on the north-west corner of Market Row. In 1937 this became Peacock's Stores Ltd., although known to most people as Peacock's Bazaar. In 1960 the corner shop became part of Brett's furniture shop.

At 2 King Street was the Domestic Bazaar Co. Ltd., selling everything for 6½d while in the Market Place was the Old Blue Coat School Bazaar, incorporating both a 1d bazaar and a 6½d bazaar, advertising 'admission free'. This building, originally a school as the name suggests, later became Nichols well-known fish restaurant.

At 12 Regent Road was another Domestic Bazaar, again selling 'any article for 6½d' and also making the bold statement 'the finest selection in the world at one price'. Why the unusual sum of 6½d was used is not clear, but in those days a half penny could buy many things. In some cases where larger items were on offer, for instance a pair of shoes, the price would be for each shoe.

Marks & Spencer's penny bazaar at 65 George Street, which opened in 1911. An open fronted walk in store.

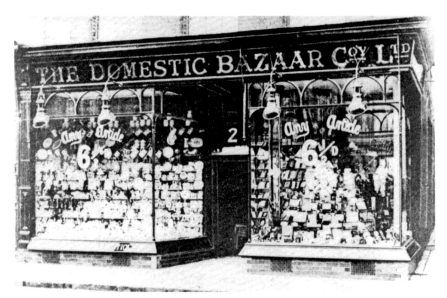

The Domestic Bazaar, 2 King Street, selling any article for 6½d.

Another 6½d bazaar, this one at 12 Regent Road, seen here in 1904.

In both these shops note the lights to illuminate the goods in the windows are outside the shop. This was common at this time as it was considered too dangerous to have gas or the new electric lights inside. Not many shops had electricity at this time

The Old Blue Coat
School bazaar on the
corner of Theatre Plain
and the Market Place. To
the right can be seen the
old Theatre Royal. This
photograph was taken in
July 1907.
In 1972 the Market Gates
shopping centre was built
on the site of the old
bazaar.

The Regent Road store of Woolworth & Co in 1937 with goods piled high in
the windows, all for 6d. This is now the site of McDonalds and Spud U Like.

From the 1920s a bazaar was to be found at 15 Market Place, next to Norman's furniture store. Run by Daniel Mason Southey, this bazaar remained open until the outbreak of the Second World War when, like many other shops in the town, it closed its doors. Throughout the 1950s and 60s this shop was a launderette and in the 1970s became Telefusion, a TV rental company. Almost sixty years after the original bazaar closed, a discount store called Essential Items opened at 15 Market Place, a modern day version of the old bazaars. Today this is a bookmaker's.

Left: The Pound Crazy shop at 19 Market Place in 2008, one of the many such outlets in the town. Seen here at Christmas time this shop later became a 97p shop in an effort to undercut its competitors. The shop closed in early 2010.

Below: the banner that replaced the Pound Crazy sign for a few months. A modern version of the 1d bazaar.

A page from a catalogue produced by Fielding's in the 1920s. In 1909 Thomas Fielding opened a jeweller's shop at 129 King Street and by 1911 this had become Fieldings Ltd, selling cycles and phonographs. In the 1920s the firm moved to 18 King Street and opened another shop at 35 Market Row. The King Street shop was damaged in the war and did not reopen. The Market Row shop expanded to number 36 becoming one of the leading cycle shops in the town. The shop closed in 1973.

44

KING STREET
and
REGENT STREET

King Street runs from the Market Place to Friars Lane and was at one time the main shopping street in the town. The street was formed when buildings were erected on the eastern side towards the end of the seventeenth century. Until then the land between the medieval town wall and what is now the western side of King Street was an open space, the dene side, from the market to Friars Lane, part of the medieval defences of the town, later used by the ropemakers and others who needed an open space for their work. As the population of the town increased and there was more demand for housing in the limited space available within the town walls this open area was developed; with St George's Church built half way along, in 1714. The street was named King's Street after the visit of Charles II in September 1671 but, following the building of St George's, a part of the street was renamed for a short time as Chapel Street. It soon became a fashionable place to live with large properties inhabited by some of the town's most wealthy citizens. Thomas Penrice was one of these wealthy townsmen, building a large house midway along the street, a site that is today Christchurch.

In the nineteenth century the ground floors of most of the residential properties were converted into shops and it became one of the most popular shopping areas in the town. Shops of all descriptions were to be found, from the large department stores like Arnolds and Bonings at the northern end of the street, to the smaller and more specialised shops in the southern half.

This is one of the earliest photographs of King Street, taken before 1860 looking south from the Market Place. On the left, known for many years as Burton's Corner, (but not a name taken from the well-known tailoring firm that has traded there for many years), is the house and shop of William Livingston, draper, and next to that the large three storey house of Samuel Crickmer Burton, a solicitor. At numbers 3 and 4 was the grocery shop of James Burton and at number 5 the shop of Biddlecombe and Boning, linen and woollen drapers.

On the right of the picture the second projecting bay belongs to John Nall the printer, a business which later was to become Jarrolds. The lamp, which advertises 'Concerts every Evening' is outside a public house known as the Elephant & Castle, which later became the Market Distillery or Red House, now part of Palmers department store.

In the foreground is a raised street crossing, a pathway enabling ladies in long sweeping dresses to cross the street avoiding the mud and dirt that was a problem when all traffic was horse-drawn and before the streets were paved.

Shoppers in King Street on a summer's day in the 1920s . Boning's store, at 2,3, 4, and 5 King Street, was taken over in May 1932 by Marks & Spencer and later rebuilt after war-time bombing. On the right is Johnson's restaurant.

(Alec McEwen)

Below: one of the departments in Boning Bros. *c.*1900.

A Bonings advert in November 1923.

The northern end of King Street in the 1950s. On the left is Matthes first floor restaurant, which before the war was Hills. On the right is the window of Montague Burton, tailors, and next to that Halfords and John Collier the tailors. Matthes closed in 1978.

Tom Green's Corner. Tom Green traded here from 1900 until 1988. Today this is Greenwoods.

King Street shops included Carr's the drapers, later to become the well-known shop of Skippings, a fine Grade II listed building, now unfortunately boarded up. This is just one of the many buildings, on both sides of King Street, that are considered architecturally important and are Grade II listed.

Other well-known names that have traded in the street include Fieldings, Halfords, International Stores, Crowes house furnishers, Fifty Shilling Tailors, Peck's Pie shop and Matthes the bakers. Wolsey & Wolsey, at 15 and 16, were established in 1910 and were piano and organ merchants. They had a piano factory in Albion Road, known as Wolsey Hall. From 1947 this became Turners shoe shop for many years.

Just off the Market Place, at numbers 2, 3, 4, and 5 King Street was the large department store of Biddlecombe & Boning, founded in the 1850s as a single shop at number 5. In 1903 this became Boning Brothers, one of the largest stores in the town at that time. In May 1932 the family firm was taken over by Marks & Spencer who had previously traded in George Street since 1911. The store was extended in 1937 but in April 1941 it was completely destroyed by bombing and, in 1946 when the war was over, Marks & Spencer opened a temporary store in the old Plaza cinema in the Market Place. They traded there until their King Street premises were rebuilt, opening in March 1952.

A name that was familiar in King Street for many years was that of Tom Green, hatter and hosier, who started trading in 1886. In 1900 Tom Green moved to a shop on the corner with Regent Road that had previously been Millers Photographic Studio. The photography business moved to the rear of the premises, with a frontage onto Regent Road but known as 14A King Street. In the 1970s this became a branch of Matthes, the Gorleston bakers. The corner shop became known as 'Tom Green's Corner', a well-known meeting point for Yarmouth people and the name soon appeared over the corner doorway. Tom Green also had a shop in the Marine Arcade, described earlier. The King Street shop continued until 1988; then taken over by Greenwoods.

The shoe shop of Pocock Brothers at 173 King Street, on the corner of Row 74 c.1900. The shop was taken over by Freeman, Hardy and Willis in 1910 and in 1926 the adjacent row was taken into the new Central Arcade. There was a shoe shop on this site, the northern corner of the Arcade, for over 120 years until Shoe Express closed in recent years.

From 1925 until 1964 Pearks Dairy and Provision Stores could be found at 160 King Street, between Rows 89 and 90. Pearks also had a branch in Market Row in the 1920s. The posters on the wall of Row 89 advertise dancing at the Britannia Pier and a variety show at the Hippodrome. This building is the oldest in King Street, and the only timber-framed building left in the town, dating from the sixteenth century. Today it is a Thai restaurant. *(Glenda Wells)*

Number 42 King Street is today King's Wine Bar but in the 1970s this was the town's first frozen food shop, Igloo. Opened in 1972 the shop is here selling frozen cod or haddock at 15p per pound.

In 1874 this fine building at 133 King Street was a college for ladies, but by 1886 it had become a carpet and furniture shop owned by Mr W Bartram. By 1894 it was George Carr's drapery shop as seen here.
From 1908 until 1997 it was Skippings.
This listed building has remained empty since then.

Halls butcher's shop at 123 King Street in 1906, the meat hanging in the open shop front.
This was one of the many buildings in the southern half of King Street demolished following bomb damage in the Second World War.

The Star Supply Stores, seen here in 1934, was at 111 King Street from 1925 until 1969. It then became the International Stores. The shop stood next to the Old White Lion public house

Regent Street was created in 1813 when a lot of property, including Rows 68 and 69, was demolished to make a new street between King Street and the Quay. When it was opened in September that year it was a residential street, with some elegant facades protected by iron railings. Businessmen living in the street soon began to establish offices within their properties, including several insurance companies. As the street was close to the town centre, shops inevitably followed. One of the earliest shops was that of James Baird, his shoe shop at number 11 opening in 1862 and still trading in the 1980s. In 1863 Valentine Cross had a chemist shop on the corner with Howard Street South which, in 1894, became Boots the Chemist, their first shop in the town. In 1870 the Corn Exchange was demolished and replaced by a new Post Office. In 1914 the adjacent corner shop of Beazor the antique dealer was demolished, and a new enlarged Post Office erected on the Hall Quay corner.

Regent Street from Hall Quay. On the left is the corner shop of Beazor, the furniture, china and curio dealer. This property was rebuilt in 1912 as the Post Office, now converted to residential use.

Thomas Lamb was a watchmaker at 18 Regent Street, next to the Post Office.
This is a typical example of how the private houses in Regent Street slowly became retail shops.
Standing outside the shop is Elizabeth Sophia Lamb.

(Peter Hellingsworth)

Bowers & Barr were established in 1890. Still trading today they are one of the longest established firms in the town. This photograph shows their shop at 24 Regent Street. Today this is the office of Alfred's, the estate agents.

(Peter Jones)

The tobacconist shop of Strickland's, 37 Regent Street. This closed in 1973. Today it is a jeweller's shop.

The Lodge Baked Potato, 40 Regent Street, seen here in 1970, was one of the first fast-food outlets in the town centre. From 1929 until 1966 this was the shop of Carr & Carr, at first gramophone and then radio and television dealers. The shop had an unusual concave glass window which gave the impression there was no glass between the goods on display and the outside pavement. In 1969 it became the Golden Egg restaurant. The Lodge closed in 1972 and it became a branch of Dorothy Perkins. Today this is an insurance office.

TOWN CENTRE

The Market Place, one of the largest in the country, has always been the centre of trade in the town. In earlier times many goods not usually available in the town were brought in and traded at the twice yearly fairs but as trading developed and goods became available from alternative sources these fairs slowly became pleasure fairs, one of which is still held annually in Easter week.

As described in an earlier chapter fresh produce for the townsfolk has always been supplied either from the town's market gardens, or by market gardeners and small farmers from the surrounding villages, who set up their stalls on the traditional market days of Wednesday and Saturday. As trade developed from the late seventeenth century the buildings surrounding the market became workshops and retail outlets, from where a large variety of goods were available. For many years the sale of meat was restricted to the eastern side of the market, the 'flesh shambles', and was not allowed to be sold in any other part of the town. Country butchers were, however, allowed to sell from their stalls on market days. In recent years the number of country stallholders has decreased as they are replaced by stalls selling a wide variety of household goods and clothes. The game dealers of the nineteenth century, where rabbits, pheasants and many other types of game were available have disappeared completely.

Shopkeepers in and around the market benefited from the many public events held there. In 1820, to celebrate the coronation of George IV, a whole ox was roasted in the Market Place, no doubt drawing a large crowd of potential customers. Public celebrations were held on occasions of national events such as coronations.

This engraving, dated 1860, shows market traders 'sitting the market' in their sentry-like shelters, each with their name at the top. Their produce is displayed on boxes in front of them.
This was a common scene on the market in the mid nineteenth century.

Market gardeners brought their produce to market in large wicker baskets known as 'skeps'. Many did not have stalls and sold directly from the skeps.

Above: the game stall of Thomas Edmonds with rabbits, pheasants, partridges and other game in abundance. This type of market trader is not seen today.
(Peter Allard)
Below: The stall of a country market gardener selling fruit and vegetables on Yarmouth market in 1971.

The northern end of the market in the 1920s. By now the country produce stalls had been supplemented by stalls selling household items and clothing. This trend was to slowly continue to the present day, when the produce stalls now only occupy a small part of the market.

LEACH & SON

Market Place & King Street

TEL. 240   TEL. 418

SPECIAL SHOW

OF

Table & Hanging

LAMPS

HALL'S DISTEMPER

ALL SHADES IN STOCK

The hardware business of Leach & Son traded from 20 and 21 Market Place for over one hundred years before closing its doors in 1995. This advertisement is from 1923. Distemper was the forerunner of today's emulsion paint.

Both pictures on this page show 41 and 42 Market Place. The shops of Mr S Randell (left) were known as Norfolk House and Waterloo House, the frontages of both surmounted by large model ships. Known as 'The Tailor King' Randell had been in business since the 1860s and advertised his Market Place shops as 'the finest emporium of the clothing trade in Yarmouth'. Number 42 later became H Samuel the jeweller.

By the 1920s both 41 and 42 Market Place had become the men's department of Palmers ever-increasing department store. This men's department was separated from the main store at this time by the Distillery public house, at number 40, just visible on the right of the photograph.

H Samuel's first shop in Yarmouth was at 42 Market Place, seen on the previous page as Randells the outfitters. A watch for 4/9 (24p) and a solid gold locket for 10/6 (52p). This later became part of Palmers department store.

The entrance to Market Row in May 1971. Traffic ran in a clockwise direction round the market, hence the pedestrian crossing. Hepworth's on the right, with the Ventura Restaurant above and Foster's on the left.

In the early nineteenth century the west side of the market was described as '*a range of very fine shops, many of them exhibiting a large and fashionable assortment of goods, the proprietors of which are exceedingly attentive and obliging.*' These shops included names such as Normans, a business founded by Simon Norman, a cabinet maker, in 1821 in Howard Street, and who had moved to 14 Market Place by 1859. In 1904 the shop was rebuilt, taking in the adjacent number 13 and in the 1920s the showroom was again enlarged.

Another well-known family business which traded in the Market Place was Leach & Son. Opening in 1868 as an ironmongers the firm had another branch in King Street which was opened to cater for trade with the fishing industry. The business expanded into window glass and had an oil, colour, lamp and paint warehouse. The trade in window glass was extensive and continued until the 1960s when specialist suppliers took over. Domestic hardware, garden requisites, tools and decorating supplies became the backbone of Leach's trade. The King Street shop closed in the 1920s and the Market Place shop continued until December 1995. In 2000 the shop was rebuilt as two units which are now occupied by Millets and Savers.

In June 1837 Garwood Burton Palmer opened a drapery shop in the Market Place. The shop grew by taking in the small shops either side until eventually occupying the space between Rows 54 and 56. After 1888 it became known as Palmer Brothers and extended north of Row 54. In 1892 most of the shop was destroyed by fire, the rebuilt shop incorporating Row 54 as a covered arcade. Numbers 41 and 42 were added as a men's department and in 1962 the Red House pub, which until then had separated the shops, also became part of the store. Eventually the arcade was taken into the main store and a new frontage added. The coffee room opened in 1967.

Other large shops to open in the market were the Co-op store in 1935 and Woolworth (now Ethel Austin) in 1959, the latter on the site of the Plaza cinema.

An impressive display in the window of W Barnes & Son, high-class grocers and provision merchants. Barnes shop was on the corner of the Conge at 8 Market Place. This display is in the immediate post war years when rationing was still in force.

Barnes shop in 1935 with Row 22 on the left. This row, together with two shops and another row were demolished when the Conge was cut through into the Market Place in 1939.

The site had been a grocer's shop for more than 120 years, Barnes having taken over from Robert Bumpstead.
The business continued until 1980. Today this is a menswear shop.

A busy market day in the late 1960s showing the Tesco store on the right. This was opened in 1964 on the site of Overill's cycle shop and Savory's fruit and vegetable warehouse. The Co-op store opened in 1935.

December 1970 and the King's Own Royal Border Regiment band lead a Father Christmas procession round the Market Place to Arnold's store. The Arthur Hollis shop was opened in 1910 in a building that was the Bull Hotel. Stricklands had shops in several parts of the town.

The largest development to take place in the centre of the town was in the 1970s when the Market Gates shopping centre was built. The aerial picture, above, taken in June 1974, shows the extent of the demolition that was necessary to make way for this multi-million pound development. One of the first buildings demolished was the Fish Stall public house in 1972. Construction work began the following year and in 1974 the landmark building known as the Conservative Club in Theatre Plain was

demolished. In 1975 the multi-storey car park was completed and also that year Sainsbury's opened as the anchor store in the new covered shopping area. This shop is now Wilkinson's. Boots moved into their new shop, from King Street, in 1976.

66

April 2006 and Dixon's is about to be renamed Currys Digital but that was not to last. Another quick change in town centre shop retailers. Today this is a book shop, The Works.

Once a household name on High Streets throughout the country, Woolworths was founded in America in 1879 and grew to become one of the largest retail chains in the world. The Yarmouth store closed 5 January 2009.

First and Last. *Above:* the Elmo store at 18 Market Place which opened in 1959 as the first self-service store in the town. Elmo gave Gold Bond stamps with purchases and closed in 1972. This shop is now Specsavers.

(Glenda Wells)

Below: the last self-service store in the town centre was Tesco on Church Plain which opened in 1980 and closed in 2003. This building is now the Palace Bingo and Casino.

REGENT ROAD

Although built in Victorian times Regent Road was named after an earlier monarch, George IV, who had been Prince Regent from 1812 until 1820, during the reign of his father George III. This was one of the first roads to be constructed across the Denes from the old walled town towards the sea front, an area that had been undeveloped for hundreds of years. The first large building erected on Regent Road was the catholic church of St Mary's in 1847 and this was soon followed by large Victorian houses and terraces, forming a residential road inhabited by many of the town's leading citizens.

As the Victorian Age progressed and seaside holidays became popular among the middle and upper classes, the piers were built and Great Yarmouth became a 'holiday resort'. By the 1870s Regent Road became the main 'tourist route' to the rapidly-developing Marine Parade. This was a period of great expansion in the town, new roads opening up the hitherto undeveloped Denes, allowing the town to grow towards the sea.

Several houses along Regent Road became apartments and lodgings during the holiday season while others gradually converted their ground floor rooms into retail outlets, selling goods aimed at the rapidly-developing holiday industry. It was not, however, until the 1920s that shops outnumbered private houses in Regent Road.

Work to pedestrianise the western end of the road began early in 1989, the section to the east of Nelson Road not being completed until some years later. Today Regent Road is at the centre of the town's holiday trade, with a large variety of shops.

Regent Road looking east in the late 1920s. The tram lines still run down the centre of the road as holidaymakers make their way to the sea front. Many properties are still residential and behind the tree on the left stands an imposing detached residence that today is the Waxworks. On the right is St John's Garage, today a bowling alley and indoor market.

The Toy House of H Davis at 31 Regent Road in 1928, a seasonal gift shop that would not look out of place today.

The Electric House in 1929, the year it was opened. The Corporation owned the power station and was responsible for electricity supplies to the town and surrounding district. All domestic electrical goods such as kettles and cookers could be hired or bought at Electric House.

A window display at the Electric House in July 1936, using the latest in electrical appliances to advertise the film *Things to Come,* then showing at the Empire cinema.

Two fish and chip shops in Regent Road in 1953. On the left is Thomas Seymour's shop with a sign above it proclaiming *'established 1948 and NO connection with next door'*. Cod and chips costs 1/- or 1/3, skate and chips costs 1/9. Tea 3d, coffee 4d and a buttered roll 2d. Today the Britannia is still a restaurant while the Neptune has become a gift shop.

Restaurants on the south side of Regent Road in the 1920s. The board advertises 1/- dinners, with a cut from the joint and two veg, Yorkshire pudding followed by bread and cheese. Pot of tea 5d.

Sutton's Bloater Depot on the corner of Regent Road and Alexandra Road
combined rock making with a shop where a box of bloaters or kippers could
be posted to anywhere in the UK. Each year thousands of small wooden boxes,
made at the front of the shop, were posted from the town, the Post Office
making special collections because of the quantity.
Below: the rock making factory inside the shop.

Currys, whose shop was at the town end of Regent Road, advertising their toys for the 1953 Christmas in the Yarmouth Mercury.
No credit cards in the 1950s but customers could purchase larger items, such as bicycles, on 'easy terms' or 'hire purchase' with a small deposit.

A MISCELLANY OF SHOPS

Small individual shops are fast disappearing from the nations streets. At one time, before the advent of the large national chains and out-of-town shopping centres, the small shop (or corner store) was the backbone of the retail trade. Away from the main shopping areas the residential districts always had their local shops. Many still exist; small family businesses that have withstood the test of time, but many others have closed and been converted into houses. The recession of recent years has also had a big impact on small businesses.

In the nineteenth century the densely-populated row area of the town was served by the many small shops in George Street, Howard Street and Middlegate Street. In these narrow streets shops selling goods of all descriptions could be found, some very small establishments with ancient bow windows that had served the local population for over a hundred years. Many of these lasted until the middle of the twentieth century when the war time destruction reduced much of the town centre to ruins. As the town was redeveloped with new housing the shops were not replaced.

In the Newtown area, developed with Victorian terrace housing, corner shops were to be found at the end of almost every road. Many of these corner shops have closed in recent years, the buildings being converted for residential use.

This section of the book illustrates just a few of the small shops that have traded in the town over the years, some of which have closed recently, others have been closed for many years. Not laid out in any particular order the images show a great variety of shops in many parts of the town.

Shops of all descriptions were to be found in Howard Street. The Arcade Stores of Downing, seen here in the 1930s, was at 9 Howard Street South, next door to the mineral water factory of Hunt's. The site is now Palmers car park.

(Glenda Wells)

Although most of Howard Street has disappeared under redevelopment schemes over the years this small northern section still exists.
Bartram's shoe shop, established for many years at 1 Howard Street North, is seen here in the 1970s and adjacent is Tates Take-Away and Coffee Lounge which later became Pedro's. Today this is known as the Private Shop, on the corner with St Francis Way.

(Glenda Wells)

76

The Antiquarian book shop of David Ferrow, 77 Howard Street.
This haven for local book collectors and literary buffs closed on 23 July 2005
after 65 years of business. David Ferrow *(inset below)* began his long career by
opening his first shop in King Street in 1940. The business moved to Howard
Street in 1952 and he became an internationally-known book dealer.

(Peter Allard)

Seen here in 1971 is the derelict shop of George Edwards, 79 Howard Street South, fishmonger. Earlier Edwards had been a greengrocer and fruiterer but this was a shop with a dark side to its history. On 18 November 1844 this was the scene of the murder of Harriet Chandler, a 41 year old widow who ran the shop as a general store. Her body was discovered behind the shop counter, her head bashed in and her throat cut. After a trial three accused men were found not guilty and released but a few months later another suspect, Samuel Yarham, was accused of the murder. The second trial convicted Yarham and he was hanged on 11 April 1846 at Norwich Castle, the last public execution in Norwich, watched by an estimated 30,000 people. It was reported that 1,500 people travelled from the town to Norwich by train to witness the execution.

To the right of the picture can be seen the shop of Kelfs Ltd, house furnishers. Kelfs closed in 1973, the buildings being demolished the following year. The site of these shops is now a car park.

The newsagents shop of W H Easto at 172 Middlegate Street in the 1920s. On the left of the picture is Row 92 and the wall of the Unitarian chapel.

After war time bombing Easto's had moved to 161 Middlegate Street. In 1957 the newsagents were on the move again, to the opposite side of the road as these buildings were due for demolition. Today this is the open area leading to the Central Library, between the Tolhouse and the Salvation Army.

Right: The butcher shop of W & G Mays at 56 Middlegate Street in the 1890s, with an interesting window display of six pigs.
This shop was on the east side of the street and Row 130 can be seen on the left. The butcher's shop was here until it became another victim of bombing during the Second World War.

Naunton & Aitken, oil merchants and hardware stores, 57 & 58 George Street in the 1920s. To the right of the shop is Row 50, now the northern pavement of Stonecutters Way.

John Harvey, baker, with his staff outside 98 & 99 South Market Road in the 1920s. Advertised here for his 'fancy biscuits and high class chocolates' the site of this shop is now part the Market Gates Shopping Centre.

(Peter Jones)

62 South Market Road *c.*1912 when it was Greoge Sheldon's bakery. In the 1920s this became Thomas Richards boot stores.

Today this is still a shoe shop (*inset*) now run by B & C Prescott. At one time there were many boot and shoe repairers but today Mr Prescott is the last traditional shoe mender in the town.

Smith's Hardware Stores, South Market Road. Before the advent of the large DIY stores the small hardware shops supplied everything the householder could need, from Distemper, the forerunner of emulsion paint, to tin baths of all sizes and garden requirements.

Southeys leather shop in Market Gates, on the corner with Fish Street, was one of the last shops to be demolished as the new shopping centre was being developed in 1972. This had previously been Pull's the saddlers.

The area known as Market Gates was originally the Fish Market, and several fish shops could still be found there into the 20th century. This one, at 1 & 2 Market Gates, later became Carr's and then Strickland's newsagents. Between this shop and the leather shop on the previous page was a shop which sold horse meat, belonging to Frosdick's the horse slaughters.

The shops of Alfred Mack, ironmonger, and William Redgrave, grocer, at 11 and 12 Blackfriars Road in 1906.
There were several shops in Blackfriars Road, serving a large residential area, many of the houses backing onto the town wall. Today large areas have been cleared and redeveloped and many of the shops demolished or, like these, converted into residential use.

The butcher's shop of W J Mays, 97 Blackfriars Road, was built in front of a house adjacent to the SE Tower. Today the shop still exists and is a mini-mart.

Float number 71 in the 1923 Carnival was entered by Mays. At this time they had another shop in Middlegate Street. Many of the towns traders entered floats in what was the town's first carnival.

Seen here in the 1930s is the greengrocer's shop of J W Balls at 98 and 99 Blackfriars Road. This property, to the north of the SE Tower, was demolished when the area against the town wall was cleared in 1972.

(Peter Jones)

A pub which was also a grocer's shop. The Recruiting Sergeant on Alma Road, pictured here in June 1901. Here Louisa Wade made and sold her well-known Dudely Wade's Toffee.

Today the pub is known as The Recruit

The Ham & Beef shop of Harry Greenacre, 158 Nelson Road Central,
*c.*1910.The shop, next to the Great Eastern public house, had closed by the
1920s but a passage beside the shop was known as Greenacre's Passage for
many years. Greenacre's was a forerunner of today's take-away shops.

(Peter Jones)

Herbert Butler, fishmonger, 23 St Nicholas Road. The site of this shop is now
part of Sainsbury's car park.

Ernest Watts, hairdresser and tobacconist shop, 36 St Peter's Road in 1908.
This shop, on the junction with Napoleon Place, also offered Hot Sea Water Baths to visitors seeking to attempt to benefit from the acclaimed medicinal qualities of sea water.
Today this shop is a Chinese take-away.

(Peter Jones)

Doughty's, originally Doughty and Baker, ladies and gentlemen's tailors, were established at 5 Northgate Street in 1897.

When the shop, on the corner with White Horse Plain, closed it was taken over by Cox the jewellers whose business next door had been established in 1875.

(Glenda Wells)

Joseph Reeve's bakery at 14 Camden Road, on the corner with Pier Place. This was claimed to be the site of Dickens Peggotty's Hut. On the bakery wall was an inscription linking the bakery with the book David Copperfield.
"Yon's our house Master Davy".
He decided in favour of a nice little brown loaf.
Today the site of this shop is a car park on the corner of Pier Place.

Another bakery, this one at 21 Northgate Street. George Arthur Bales and his staff, including the delivery man, outside the bakery in 1917. Bales had taken over from Rolling *c.*1912. Today this shop retains one of the few original Victorian shop façades in the town.

The pork butchers, F Base & Sons, 131 Mill Road in 1922.
Today this is a second-hand furniture shop.

(Glenda Wells)

The Cobholm Island Post Office on Mill Road, on the corner with Cobholm
Road. Although today the post office has gone, a shop remains on the site with
a letter box nearby.

(Peter Allard)

Goodram's Stores, 45 High Mill Road, on the corner with Gatacre Road.
The window display advertises Dawson's cake mixture *"as partaken of by
H.R.H. Princess Mary during her visit to Melton Lodge"*. This was when the
royal visitor opened the children's home in January 1921.

(Peter Jones)

On the opposite corner of Gatacre Road was the wool shop of Olivettes, 46
High Mill Road. This opened in 1962, the shop having previously been that of
E & W Jones, the drapers.   *(Michael Harvey)*

GORLESTON

In the nineteenth century Gorleston was still a small agricultural and fishing community, the commercial centre of which was the small Market Place, situated on the land in front of the Feathers Inn. The main shopping areas developed as the High Street, and later, Bells Road. From the beginning of the twentieth century the opening of the Pavilion, and other amenities at the foot of the cliffs, brought an increasing number of summer visitors to Gorleston and it became a seaside resort.

The post war years saw a rapid increase in the resident population as large new housing estates, such as the Magdalen Estate and the Cliff Park Estate, were built. Although a few shops were built in these new residential areas the main shopping areas remained the High Street and Bells Road.

For over 70 years the best known and largest grocers in Gorleston were Bussey's, who had shops in both Bells Road and the High Street. This firm finally closed in 1968. In May 1971 a new shopping area opened in the High Street, named the Precinct. The largest shop in this new development was Hollis's Discount Supermarket, now Wilkinson's. The site of the Coliseum cinema was redeveloped in 1971 with two shops, Boots and Liptons. The Grove Glade Indoor Shopping Hall later opened where Liptons had been. This closed in 1995 and is now Iceland.

The number of shops in Bells Road has declined and now the High Street is the principal shopping area. The first national supermarket to open in Gorleston was Fine Fare in the High Street in 1964. In 1987 this became QD Stores. Somerfield, now Morrison's, later opened at the end of Baker Street.

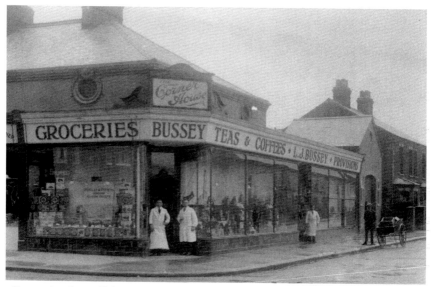

Bussey's, the well-known Gorleston grocers, at 134 Bells Road, on the corner with Springfield Road, closed at the beginning of the Second World War. Bussey's also had a shop in the High Street, which closed in 1968.

(Peter Jones)

Another well-known business in Bells Road in the 1930s was Eagle & Green's drapery shop at numbers 52 and 54. In 1965 this became Olivettes wool shop; today the shop is a pet grooming salon.

(Peter Jones)

Coopers, on the corner of Cliff Hill and Englands Lane, was established in
1877 by Mr A J Cooper. The shop retained the name although taken over in
1944 by Mr Adcock and later by Clifford Bedson. By 1980 the shop
specialised in high quality china and porcelain, still known as Coopers of
Gorleston 'for beautiful things'. The last owner was artistic and painted many
murals on the shop (*inset*). After closing in 2004 it is now a private house.

(Julie Grint)

Next door to the above shop, at 1 Englands Lane was Herbert Watts the
hairdresser, whose shop is seen here decorated for the 1923 Carnival.

(The Watts Family)

Tom Allard outside his Radio & Music Salon , 42 Bells Road, on the corner with North Road, in 1935. The window advertises several names that have disappeared from the radio scene, such as Marconi, Cossor and Ekco. Today this shop is an Estate Agents.   *(Peter Allard)*

John Wright's gentlemen's outfitters shop was at 57 High Street in the 1930s. By the 1950s this was a fishmongers but today the property has been converted into a private house.

(Peter Jones)

Above: The hardware shop, and staff, of Philip Hammond on the corner of
Lowestoft Road and Church Lane *c*.1905.
The business later moved to 138 High Street, where Hammond converted
Rope's farmhouse into a hardware shop.
Below: By the 1970s the business had been taken over by Coopers.
The old farmhouse can be seen behind the modern shop extension.

Gorleston High Street *c.* 1900. The open-top horse drawn trams ran from the foot of the Haven Bridge to Gorleston from 1875 until replaced by electric trams in 1905. On the right is the shop of the Yarmouth Industrial Cooperative Society Ltd, now rebuilt and the Gorleston Post Office. Beyond that, with the striped blind, is the confectionery shop of Benjamin Wright, now a barber's shop. The white blind shields the windows of Bussey's the grocers. On the opposite side of the road Barclays Bank was built on the site of the garden the tram is passing, on the corner of Palmer Road.

The corner of High Street and Church Lane was known for many years as Norton's Corner. Seen here in 1968 after the tobacconist shop, and the adjacent Gorleston Garden Shop, which had earlier been Arthur Hollis the corn merchant, had closed. This is now the site of Lloyds TSB.

(Peter Allard)

Above: Reeve's the leather merchants at 127 High Street next to the Feathers Inn *c.*1915. Today this, and the adjacent shop, form Blockbuster, the video rental store.

Left: By 1922 the shop had become a branch of Plattens, the outfitters, whose main shop was in Broad Row, Great Yarmouth.

97

Clowes Stores at 99 & 100 High Street. In the 1930s Clowes, high class grocers, also had shops in Bells Road and at Hall Quay, Great Yarmouth. The shop is today Magic City Amusements.

Stone's the tobacconist and sweet shop, at 103 High Street, closed in 1954. This picture shows the shop in 1928. It is now Brief Encounters.

(Peter Jones)

Beckett & Pitcher's grocery shop at 140 High Street closed in 1971, remaining empty for several years. This picture was taken in 1976.

(Peter Allard)

The Gorleston branch of Woolworth & Co opened in Lowestoft Road in 1932 and closed in 1974.

The grocery shop of Claud Millichamp, 153 Beccles Road in the 1950s.
This shop was on the corner with Frederick Road.

(Peter Jones)

For many years Field's the gentlemen's outfitters was a well-known name in Gorleston. This advertisement, for their shop at 58 Bells Road, on the corner with Upper Cliff Road, is from 1969.

The Village Shop

The village shop, like its counterpart in urban areas, the corner shop, is becoming increasingly rare. Every year hundreds close and many small villages now have no shops at all. There are many reasons for this including the declining village populations, the increase in car ownership and increased rural public transport. These facts, combined with the competition from the large supermarket chains, entice country dwellers into the towns where a larger range of goods is readily available.

By the 1860s there was at least one general store in every sizable village, most of them run by women, to supplement the household income. Sometimes the shop would be combined with another line of business such as a baker, shoemaker or blacksmith. Most village shops were simply the front room of a private house, few were purpose built. These were family-run businesses where service was on a very personal level, the shopkeeper knowing the customers by name. A vast range of goods were stocked but few items were pre-packed, the

shopkeeper bought in bulk and packaged items in smaller quantities as required. Opening hours were long, six days a week and often until late into the evening. It was not until the Shop Act of 1912 that half day closing on Wednesdays was brought in.

By the beginning of the twentieth century the general store had become established as an essential element in village life, the focal point of the community. A delivery service was provided, either by handcart, trade cycle or horse-drawn van or cart to more remote cottages, or to nearby villages where there was no shop. Many village stores incorporated a drapery section and a hardware section. Some found it beneficial to include a post office while others sold bicycles and a few, such as Hemsby, had a petrol pump for the lucky few local car owners.

In larger villages, such as Caister, there were more specialised small shops. The draper, grocer, greengrocer and newsagent were often separate businesses. Here again the availability of public transport into the nearby town: trains from 1877, electric trams from 1907 and then the motor car led to the decline and eventual closure of many of these small shops. By the 1930s small shops were finding it difficult to compete with the competition from the large town stores and the new mail order service.

A reconstructed village shop at the Gressenhall Rural Life Museum.

Today, where a village shop has survived, it has adapted to modern retailing practices, often becoming a mini-supermarket, emulating its larger rivals in the town. Although today much of the personal service has gone the village store still provides an essential service.

The traditional village store of the inter-war years is now only to be seen in museum reconstructions.

On Station Road at Ormesby was the grocery shop of Charles Freeman, seen here in the 1920s. Mr Freeman retired in 1946, the shop continuing in new ownership until *c.*1966 when it was rebuilt, becoming a MACE shop.

(Helen Gallaway)

Helen Gallaway, daughter of Charles Freeman, was brought up in the above shop and remembers it as it was in the 1930s.

"The floor of brick red stone pamments is well worn by many feet. The counter runs across the shop—dark brown mahogany, glowing warmly and lovingly polished. On one side is a wall of biscuit tins with long forgotten names, Pat-a-Cake, Thin Arrowroot and Petit Beurre. On the other a display of tinned goods and jars in various shapes and sizes. Behind is an alcove stacked up with Germolene, Beechams Pills, Eno's Fruit Salts, leather boot laces, balls of string, elastic, cards of studs and of pot menders. Behind the counter are the glass sweet jars filled with aniseed balls, gobstoppers and many other sweets, all ready to be weighed on the brass scales. On the back wall are the tall green canisters full of tea and below deep wooden draws for sugar, rasins, currants and peel. The big round red cheese has been skinned, ready to be cut, and the bacon ready to be sliced to any thickness the customer requires. In front of the counter are piles of oranges, apples, lemons and bananas. A wooden barrel, filled with small pieces of cork, contains the sweet green grapes. On the floor boxes ready to be delivered to the outlying cottages by our horse-drawn van."

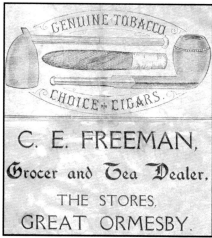

C. E. FREEMAN,

Grocer and Tea Dealer,

THE STORES,

GREAT ORMESBY.

Above is the horse-drawn delivery cart of Freeman's. Weekly deliveries were made to houses in Scratby and California, where there were no shops, and to a few customers in the neighbouring village of Filby.

(Helen Gallaway)

John Freeman, on the left, ran a general store which later became a hardware shop at Filby Lane, Ormesby. This was at the opposite end of the village green to his father's shop seen on the previous page.

(Joan Fletcher)

Freemans shop was demolished in the 1960s and a new development of three shops was built on the Station Road site. The shop facing Station Road was a MACE shop known as Ormesby Stores which, like many village shops that had survived into the 60s had to incorporate the latest development in shopping, self-service.

Today this shop has been divided into two separate units, a hairdressers and a bakery.

In West Road was another general store, draper and newsagent, owned by Joe Hitcham. In the 1960s this was taken over by the Fletchers and is today a modern village shop complete with laundrette, known as Stonehouse Stores.

(Joan Fletcher)

105

In Filby the Archway Stores, at the eastern end of the village, closed in the 1960s and was demolished c.1972, the last shopkeepers being Mr and Mrs Mudge. Houses were built on the site in 1975.

(The Filby Archive)

At the other end of the village was the post office and general store, on the corner of Thrigby Road. The post office closed here in 1963, the last postmistress being Miss Phyllis English. The building remained as a shop for several years but today is a private house.

(The Filby Archive)

Allard's general stores at Rollesby was another grocer's to incorporate a drapery department. Today this much altered shop, on the main road, is a hair and beauty shop called Serenity.

Hemsby post office and village general store, run for two generations by the Church family. This was one of the few village stores to supply petrol to the 1930s motorists, the hand-cranked Esso pump can be seen on the right.

(Peter Jones)

The greengrocer shop of Leslie England in Caister High Street. Today this is a carpet shop. In the background can be seen the workshop of the village basket maker George Lawrence.

On the opposite side of Caister High Street was the millinery and drapery shop of Miss Sarah Humphrey. This shop was demolished in 1968 as part of a road widening scheme through this narrow part of the village.

The general store of Mrs Postle, seen here with her daughter, in Beach Road at Caister, in the 1920s. Today this is the Beach Road Chippy.

Ursula Hunt in the doorway of her corner shop in Caister High Street in the 1930s, a small shop selling grocery, sweets and tobacco. In a period when nearly everybody smoked, cigarettes and tobacco were available in most shops of this type.

Today this shop is a Co-op chemist on the corner of Beach Road and the High Street.

Loading up for the deliveries at the Caister branch of Arthur Hollis's corn, flour and seed stores in the 1930s. Hollis's main store was in Great Yarmouth Market Place. Today this shop is a funeral director's.

A fine selection of meat displayed in the window of Charles Hunn's butcher's shop in Yarmouth Road, Caister. All the staff, including the delivery boy, are in this picture, taken in 1933. This later became Rackham's butchers and closed in 1998. Today it is a florists, Thistle & Thorne.

Joseph Haylett standing outside
his tobacconist shop in Tan Lane
in the 1930s.
Like many of the small shops in
Caister this has now been
converted into a private house.

A small lock-up shop at 1A Yarmouth
Road, one of two such shops built as
part of the Caister Council Hall.
In 1937 it became Ivy's Handy Shop,
selling a wide range of small bits and
pieces, run by Miss Rose Thurley,
seen here in the doorway.

A busy summer scene in Yarmouth Road, Caister in 1975.
The post office moved into Offords in 1987, the shop then became a branch of
the TSB bank. It is now a fast food take-away. The self-service store has been
a branch of the Co-op since the 1920s.

The sweet and cigarette counter in Offords, Yarmouth Road, taken only a short time before decimalisation day in 1971. Olivier cigarettes are priced at 3/4 (17p) for 20.